STUDY SKILLS FOR SUCCESS

How to learn effectively

William M. Saleebey, Ph.D.

NATIONAL PUBLISHERS
of the Black Hills, Inc.

Published by
National Publishers
of the Black Hills, Inc.

Library of Congress Catalog Number: 81-83180

ISBN 0-935920-25-0

Printed in the United States of America
Second Printing, March 1985

DEDICATION

This book is lovingly dedicated to Mom and Dad, who made it all possible.

ACKNOWLEDGEMENTS

Many people have assisted and encouraged me along the way. I am especially grateful to Bill Vega, Vice-President of Compton Community College, who asked me to teach Study Skills in the first place, and is a close personal friend. To Clark McKowen, Instructor at Diablo Valley College, who has been so supportive of me. To my students, who helped me to formulate the ideas for this book. To Dr. Rudolph Von Burg, Chevron Chemical Corporation, for editorial assistance.

Above all, to my dear wife Christine, who was primarily responsible for the publishing of this book. She encouraged me to write it, provided many ideas along the path of revision, did all of the graphic design and illustrations, and coordinated all of the business associated with the book. Without her help, this book would have remained only a dream.

To all of these people and others too numerous to mention, I am extremely thankful.

CONTENTS

CHAPTER 3
MEMORY: AN ESSENTIAL ACADEMIC
AND LIFE SKILL

INTRODUCTION

You probably picked up this book because you want to learn things easier and remember them better. You might want to learn specific methods that will assist you in those areas. In any case, you will find numerous ideas contained in this book to get you started. I hope that you find this book enjoyable. More importantly, I hope that it starts you on the road to increased wisdom, self-awareness, and academic success.

Purpose of the book

This book is designed for any students who want to improve their study skills. It is written in a language that is easy to understand. The approach is practical, and the principles which are suggested have proven to be successful with many different types of students. The information will be most helpful to students who actually **PRACTICE** new methods and honestly assess their academic strengths and weaknesses. *IT IS NOT ENOUGH TO UNDERSTAND THE MATERIAL IN THIS BOOK. YOU NEED TO MAKE A CONTINUAL EFFORT TO IMPROVE YOUR CURRENT STUDY HABITS.*

You can use this book throughout your academic career, and even after you are finished with school. Certain topics might be especially important to you now, and others might apply later. Do not feel that you need to read this book from cover to cover. Select any topic that interests you. Skip and skim to suit *YOUR NEEDS*. You will gain many benefits from reading this book. Learning will be much more enjoyable and productive for you. Academic success will lead to success in other aspects of your life.

What makes this book unique

There have been other books written about studying. You might be interested in knowing what makes this one unique. Most of the information that you will find here is primarily the result of common sense and experience. I have taught study skills to almost every type of student (young and old, foreign born, motivated and unmotivated). Because of this extensive experience, I feel qualified to make some statements about ways to increase academic efficiency and effectiveness. Besides this teaching experience, I have been a student myself for many years and have been associated with a wide variety of students.

One thing that makes this book unique is that it is not limited to any grade level or subject matter. These principles of learning apply to almost any situation. I also realize that school and studying are not always stimulating or top priorities. I encourage you to **CREATE YOUR OWN STUDY HABITS** rather than copying those of someone else. You should accept **RESPONSIBILITY** for learning, and take control of your own education. It is up to you to learn.

As you read this, you should have a pen near you. **WRITE IN THIS BOOK**. There are activities and space provided to complete them. You will learn more if you take the time to complete each activity. In addition to completing the various activities, feel free to make any written comments in the margins. This process of writing will aid in your learning and memory of this material.

The main thing that makes this book unique is that it allows you a great deal of **FREEDOM** in selecting your study methods. But in order for you to select methods that are appropriate for you, you need to learn about yourself. In that way you can find the methods that fit your personality and needs.

Author's background, approach and perspective

I am an educational psychologist with a specialization in study skills. My background includes teaching, counseling, and consulting. In 1980 I developed an educational service called the **STUDY SKILLS SEMINAR**. The seminar has been attended by hundreds of students, teachers, counselors, parents, and working people to improve their study skills.

In addition to teaching and promoting the **STUDY SKILLS SEMINAR** through radio, television, and newspaper interviews, I was responsible for developing study skills programs in many schools and school districts. As a frequent interview guest, I had the opportunity to answer a variety of questions on call-in programs. This experience helped me to determine the major problems faced by students.

After teaching study skills using other people's ideas and materials, I decided to write a book on the subject. I have tried to make these ideas easy for you to understand and use. I will provide you with numerous practical suggestions. It is up to you to put them into practice. There is no substitute for **HARD WORK**. Learning involves dedication and effort, and can bring you much joy.

I feel that in order for you to develop study habits that will work for you, you need to do the following things:

1. Learn as much about yourself as possible.
2. Try different methods until you find ones that are effective.
3. Do not blame anyone else for your failure to learn or understand—**TAKE CONTROL OF AND RESPONSIBILITY FOR YOUR OWN EDUCATION**.
4. Develop a positive attitude toward learning. If you do, then everything will be easier and more enjoyable.
5. Be aware of your goals and priorities.

I believe that you can learn more efficiently. You are the only person who can change your habits. Good luck to you in your pursuit of knowledge. There is an exciting world awaiting you.

CHAPTER 1

CREATING THE CONDITIONS
FOR ACADEMIC SUCCESS

At the beginning of each chapter is an ***OVERVIEW***. This overview summarizes the main ideas contained in the chapter.

Overview

This chapter will discuss some of the important conditions that lead to academic success. Before we begin on our journey to wisdom, better grades, and success, let us ask the question: ***WHAT IS STUDYING?*** To study something is to examine it closely with the intention of understanding and remembering it. This activity will vary depending upon whether we are talking about math, English, history, Spanish, biology, or art. But whatever the subject or grade level, studying demands focused attention and concentration. Without those skills, our mind tends to wander to other topics. Studying sometimes demands the exclusion or postponing of other interesting topics due to time limits. Efficiency is emphasized in this chapter. It is important to develop a positive attitude toward school and learning. You should get involved deeply in the learning process, and take an active approach to your education. In addition, you need to assume an increased responsibility for learning. Organization is very important to learning. In order to increase your academic efficiency, you should learn as much as you possibly can about yourself and your various instructors.

Increasing efficiency: emphasis on results

The methods presented in this book are designed to save you time and energy. However, ***WORK*** is necessary at certain points in order to save time at others. As a student, you are "paid" with knowledge and grades on the basis of ***RESULTS*** rather than the amount of time spent studying. It doesn't do you much good to spend countless hours poring over your books if you aren't accomplishing anything. It is to your advantage to make the most efficient use of your time. You will enjoy studying if you are successful and productive.

Do you waste any time when you study? Most people do until they learn various methods to improve their efficiency. Efficiency is the ability to accomplish the most work in the shortest time with the least amount of effort. This does not mean rushing through your school work or doing it sloppily. If you want to be able to have more free time, then **READ ON**.

Think of any task that you have become an expert on after continual practice. It could be mowing the lawn, vacuuming the house, washing the dishes, or cleaning your room. I'll bet that when you first did that particular task, you tended to waste time and get frustrated. You probably didn't know the most efficient way to perform it. As time passed and you tried different methods, you became more efficient. You learned how to prepare for the task, carry it out, and take pride in your finished product. You turned a menial task into an accomplishment. You can do the same with studying. In fact, studying is similar to other jobs that you perform easily and skillfully.

Activity 1 — Description of successful activity

Think of anything that you do well. In the space provided below, describe that activity. Make a note of the steps that you went through to reach your current ability. Exactly **HOW** did you get to be an expert in that task? Is there anything about that task that you could apply to studying?

There are certain tasks that involve what seems like extra work. For example, if you are washing a car, it takes some time to make sure that all of the windows are shut tight before turning on the hose. In addition, you should have a bucket of soapy water ready before wetting the car down. This preparation will actually save you time. If you are mowing a lawn, it is helpful to clear it off before beginning to mow. A similar kind of preparation applies to studying. Certain steps will save you from wasted time and effort. If you are unwilling to take these suggested steps, then you will not improve your study efficiency.

Consider these examples. Joe is in a hurry to wash the dishes. Because of this, he doesn't take the time to rinse them before putting them in the water. All goes well until the water becomes too greasy to wash the dishes properly. He needs to take time to re-wash the greasy dishes and wait for the water to get hot again. By being in such a hurry, he actually has to spend more time than necessary on the task.

Susie is anxious to finish her math homework so she can go outside. She doesn't take the time to learn the formulas and procedures. This prevents her from completing the problems without constantly referring to the book. The main point here is as follows: If preparatory steps will make a task easier, take the time to complete them. This process will increase your *EFFICIENCY*.

You can consider school as a kind of job. Studying is a major part of your work. Many jobs pay people by the hour, regardless of the quantity or quality of their work. School "pays" you by *RESULTS*. The student who studies for ten hours and gets a C on a test is rewarded with the same grade as the student who studies for two hours and gets a C. If you can learn to master the same material in less time, it will be to your benefit. This book will show you numerous ways to increase your academic efficiency.

The importance of a positive attitude

I realize that you might not be very motivated or "turned on" by school. In fact, one reason you are reading this book is for some inspiration. I will admit that there are teachers who are boring, vague, and unfair. There are books that are difficult to read. There are subjects that you don't like or see the reason for taking. Despite these problems, you can still learn. As long as you make excuses for not learning, then you will never reach your academic potential. *YOU ARE THE ONLY PART OF THE EDUCATIONAL SYSTEM OVER WHICH YOU HAVE CONTROL!*

Some students spend much time trying to avoid studying. They could be using some of that time studying instead of complaining, worrying, or making excuses. Once you get into the *HABIT* of studying on a regular basis, you will have much more free time. Any task is easier if you approach it with a positive attitude. School is no exception.

Studying will continue to be a burden unless *YOU* do something to make it more enjoyable. Believe it or not, studying can be fun. Before you can learn effective study methods, you should become aware of your current attitude toward school. A positive, receptive attitude toward learning is necessary for developing effective study habits. If you have ever performed a difficult task, you know that a negative attitude makes the task even more difficult. On the other hand, a positive attitude can take the sting out of the most dreadful job.

Let me give you an example of what I am talking about. One job that I had was to dig post holes in very hard ground. Nothing that I have ever done in my life was so demanding, repetitious, and boring. If I continued to complain, it would have seemed even more unbearable. I made a game out of it. I divided the task into segments. I counted each hole that I dug, and then figured out how many more I had left to do. I was working with other guys, and we made it fun by joking about it. We also pretended that there was a treasure at the bottom of each hole. By making the job entertaining, I could actually forget how difficult the job was at times.

While I was attending high school and college, I worked as a funiture mover. Attitude was also very important in this job. When you are moving 25,000 pounds of household goods in a day, you need to have a positive attitude to make the task seem easier. Complaining only makes things seem heavier. I would notice how people with a positive attitude seemed to enjoy their jobs more. Instead of thinking about how heavy a certain object was, it was more beneficial to think about completing the task by a certain time. By setting **POSITIVE GOALS** and rewarding myself with a well deserved break or meal, I managed to complete even the most difficult jobs.

Mental and emotional attitudes have a tremendous influence on your ability to perform tasks. Your mind can help determine whether you succeed or fail.

Activity 2—Description of your attitude toward school

In the space below, describe your current attitude toward school. Exactly how do you feel about your teachers, classes, books, and studying? Take a few minutes to think about your attitudes and how they developed. Are there any of your attitudes that should be changed? If so, what can you do to change those that seem to be preventing you from reaching your academic potential? Is your attitude toward school similar to your attitude about other aspects of your life?

Active learning

In order to be successful in school, it is necessary to get **INVOLVED** in the material that you are studying. Learning is an **ACTIVE** process. The more that you do, the more you will learn. Think about the material, tell others about it, and write things on paper. Try to relate what you are studying to things you already know. Perhaps the least efficient way to learn is to merely sit and hope that the information sinks in.

An active approach to learning means that you question, react, practice, and use the information. You don't learn to drive a car merely by reading how it is done. The same principle applies to school: **YOU LEARN BY DOING**. You should try to use as many of your senses as possible. Try to determine which of your senses is the most powerful. For example, if you notice sounds more than the appearance of something, then try to use your hearing to assist you in the learning process.

Concentration

One of the major problems faced by students is the inability to concentrate. Our mind wanders, we think of other things, and we aren't able to focus on the material. Distractions which interfere with conentration can be divided into two major types: **INTERNAL** distractions (such as feelings, thoughts, or uncompleted tasks) and **EXTERNAL** distractions (such as noise or nature). You can learn to control both types of distractions. To do so, your desire to study must be stronger than your desire to listen to the radio or think about your friends.

One way to eliminate distractions is to try to block them out of your mind. Another way is to select an environment that is free of distractions. Perhaps the best method is to become so deeply involved in an activity that you are no longer aware of the distractions. This is done with ease by many successful people. They become totally absorbed in their work. By learning to concentrate, you will save yourself many hours that you used to daydream, worry, and become distracted.

Life consists of things that you can control and things that you cannot control. You can't control how many older brothers and sisters you have or where you were born. But you can control the volume or your radio, when you study, and your attitude. Let's take the example of household noise. You have several options if you want to study and the noise is distracting you. You could ask the other people in the house to keep the noise down. You could go into a room and shut the door. There are other possibilities, but these are enough to make the point. You might ask yourself whether it is the noise or your own ability to concentrate that is bothering you.

If you have ever had the experience of getting so involved in something that you are not distracted by anything, then you are already capable of dealing with distractions. What was happening when you were able to do this? Try to determine the exact conditions when you reached this state of concentration. Then apply or create similar conditions for studying.

You should try to reach the point where your mind is free from distractions when you sit down to study. It might help to make a list of tasks or the things that are interfering with your concentration. You should place those things in order of priority, and complete them as soon as you are able. If you are bothered more by feelings than specific tasks, you can take some time to direct your attention to those feelings. You might not be able to solve all of them at once, but at least you can work on them. You will be able to concentrate better if you accept that fact.

There are times when conflicting demands interfere with your concentration. For example, your brother wants you to go somewhere with him. Instead of taking an hour to satisfy him, you might spend more time refusing, explaining, or feeling guilty for not going with him. You need to be able to recognize the best course of action to take when you are faced with decisions and conflicts. There are some cases when it is better to postpone studying.

Taking control of your education

From the beginning of your education, you have probably been taught to do what your teachers say. For this and other reasons, it might be difficult to develop **INITIATIVE**. However, that is exactly what is necessary for you to become an independent learner. **YOU NEED TO TAKE CONTROL OF YOUR OWN EDUCATION**. This involves not waiting for your teacher to tell you when to read something, when to think about something, and how well to learn something. It is **YOU** who controls what and how much you learn. Therefore, it is to your advantage to take increased control of your learning. As soon as you determine what needs to be done in a situation, do it. You make the decisions about what and how well you need to learn something.

Finding your formula for academic success

There is more than one formula for academic success. What works for one person might not work for another. Just as actors and athletes have different styles, so too can students be successful with different approaches to studying. For example, some students are effective studying the first thing in the morning. Others need more time to become fully alert. Some students re-write their notes immediately after class, while others leave them in their original form. It is up to you to analyze yourself and develop an appropriate style of studying with which you are comfortable. You will enjoy studying more if you are responsible for selecting your own unique method. You might need to change certain aspects of your method. But those decisions will come more easily after you have determined the effects of your approach.

Activity 3 — Description of your current study environment

Describe **WHERE, WHEN, AND HOW** you currently study. Are there any changes that you could make that might improve your academic success? If so, list them in the space which is provided.

The need for self-awareness

The previous discussion and activities have emphasized an important aspect of developing effective study skills: **KNOW YOURSELF**. The more accurate information you have about yourself, the easier it will be to make the desired changes in attitudes *and* behavior. This process of becoming aware of yourself will enable you to select methods that are appropriate for you. If you don't assess yourself honestly, then positive change is unlikely. You should be thinking about what you are reading. Make an effort to apply these ideas to **YOUR SITUATION**. Don't be in a hurry to finish this book. Many of the ideas are presented in a condensed form. Because of this, you will continue to see different applications long after your first reading.

Activity 4 — Assessing your academic strengths and weaknesses

This activity is designed to get you to think about areas in which you have strengths and weaknesses. Think carefully about yourself before completing this activity. An example is provided for you.

Example

Academic Strengths	Academic Weaknesses
Listening	Note-taking
Speaking in class	Concentration
Memory	Taking tests

Academic Strengths	Academic Weaknesses

The need for organization

One of the central principles of learning and memory is **ORGANIZATION**. You need to become organized in both your personal life and with the material you are attempting to learn. Given the same amount of knowledge, the student who is organized will perform better than the student who is disorganized. You can use existing structures such as headings and outlines to become organized. In addition, you might need to create your own patterns. It is well worth your time to organize material before attempting to memorize it. This concept will appear throughout the book.

Learning about your instructors

Every teacher that you will have is a little bit different. The same work that earned you an A in one class might be considered average in another. Because of this, you should learn as much as you can about each of your teachers. What are their interests, biases, rules, and methods of grading?

Sometimes your teacher will provide you with most of the information that you need to know about him or her. In many cases it is your responsibility to determine the important aspects of their personality. I have seen students who can either make or hurt their grades because of their relationship with the teacher. There is no reason to lessen your chances for success because you fail to know your teachers.

Activity 5 — Description of instructor

Select any of your current or past instructors. Then complete the requested information. If you want, you can do the same thing for all of your teachers on separate paper.

1. What are the major rules in this class?

2. Which aspect of the subject is the instructor most interested?

3. On what basis are grades given in this class?

4. How did you learn the above information about the instructor?

If you feel satisfied with your understanding of this chapter, then try to write down the **MAJOR IDEAS** below. Then try to explain those ideas to someone else. If you are still uncertain about something, then re-read that section. After you feel that you understand the information presented in this chapter, then proceed to Chapter 2.

CHAPTER SUMMARY

1. Studying involves focused attention and concentration.
2. By increasing your academic efficiency, you can get the same work done with less time and effort.
3. A positive attitude will enable you to complete your work easier and with enjoyment.
4. An active approach to learning uses many of your senses and gets you involved in the learning process.
5. Concentration can be enhanced by eliminating both internal and external distractions.
6. If you take more control of your education you will prepare yourself to be an independent learner.
7. You need to develop your own formula for studying, based upon a knowledge of yourself.
8. Self-awareness is a key factor in learning how to study.
9. Organization is central to learning and memory.
10. It is important to learn as much as you can about each of your instructors.

Notes

CHAPTER 2

ATTENTION, NOTE-TAKING, AND MAKING THE MOST OF CLASS TIME

Overview

This chapter emphasizes the importance of learning in the classroom. Part of being an efficient student is not to waste time. The more that you learn and remember in class, the less work that you will have to do out of class. Before learning to take notes, you will need to develop the skills of paying attention and listening. There are many reasons for taking notes. However, the main function of note-taking is to provide you with a written record of what happens in class. Because our memories are imperfect, notes assist us in recalling the events of class. The main thing about taking notes is to write the main points that are made by the instructor. In order for our notes to be useful, it is important to keep them neat and organized. Note-taking is an important academic skill that will assist you greatly in learning. It is not a substitute for listening. You should learn to balance listening and writing so that you continue to hear what the teacher is saying even while you are writing. The technique of previewing will assist you in note-taking by preparing you to receive the information presented in lectures.

Reasons for taking notes

As a teacher and student, I have seen many students enter the classroom not ready to listen and take notes. They are usually unaware of how important it is to learn as much as possible in class. You need to be able to grasp the **MAIN IDEAS** of each lecture. In order to remember those and other ideas, it is helpful to take notes. **NOTES ARE FOR YOUR BENEFIT AND USE, AND DON'T NEED TO BE SEEN OR EVALUATED BY ANYONE ELSE**. The primary reasons for taking notes are as follows:

1. You will have something to refer to when you are studying.
2. You can develop a listing of main ideas expressed by the instructor.
3. You are more **ACTIVE** than you would be if you were merely sitting in class listening or daydreaming.
4. You are able to develop a kind of "handwritten textbook" which will contain the major information for a given course.
5. The act of writing aids in memory.
6. You are likely to become more involved in the subject through active listening and note-taking.
7. Taking notes tends to reduce boredom and distractions. The more you learn in class, the less work you will have outside of class. You should come to class ready to learn. It takes much practice to become an effective note-taker. You need to develop your own style. Above all, your notes should make sense to you.

The need for attention

In order to learn anything, you need to **PAY ATTENTION**. It is not enough to hear the words that are spoken by the teacher in class. You need to understand the meaning of those words and the ideas that are related to them. You go to class to learn. When you arrive in the classroom, you should put aside other aspects of your life. You will be successful in school if you learn to regularly "enter the world" of each subject that you study.

Before taking notes, you need to listen carefully to the teacher. ***NOTE-TAKING IS NOT A SUBSTITUTE FOR LISTENING***. It is only after you have learned to pay attention and listen actively that you will know what to write in your notes.

Getting the main points

The main thing that you need to know about note-taking is this: ***WRITE THE MAIN POINTS***. You are not a court reporter. With the exception of quotations, formulas, poems, speeches, and foreign languages, you don't usually need to write information word for word. Beginning note-takers often make the mistake of trying to write every word. You should try to take notes ***IN YOUR OWN WORDS***.

You might be wondering how to determine the main points from the mass of words spoken by the teacher. What kinds of ***CLUES*** does your teacher provide you regarding the main points? One obvious clue lies in ***REPETITION***. Information that is repeated tends to be more important than that which is mentioned only once. Another clue involves material that is written on the board. In some cases the teacher's tone of voice can provide information about main points. There are certain words and phrases that indicate importance. They include the following:

    most important
    especially
    remember
    this will be on the test
    central
    major
    therefore

Some teachers will give an overview prior to beginning their lecture. This overview can alert you about what to expect in terms of main points. The amount of time devoted to a topic can also tell you something about its importance. Review sessions often provide information that should be written down and remembered. Can you think of any other clues used by your teachers to indicate main points?

Paying careful attention is probably your best guide to the main points. By paying attention you can follow the development of ideas and understand the various relationships among the ideas. You should develop your own system of noting emphasis, such as stars, checks, or different colors of ink.

You probably don't pay attention equally throughout a class session. You are more alert and attentive at certain times. You should increase the intensity of your listening when you anticipate a main point. Then you can relax a bit when the teacher is off on a tangent. Your teachers will differ in terms of how strongly or obviously they indicate the main points. It is wise for you to develop a system that does not depend upon the teacher telling you what is important. In that way you will get into the **HABIT** of looking for the main points in every lecture. It is not only the quantity of studying that is important, but also where you place most emphasis. Certain things need to be learned more thoroughly than others. The effective student learns to predict which information is the most important.

Previewing

There is yet another way to become aware of the major ideas in a given subject. That is to **PREVIEW** the material before coming to class. For example, if the teacher is going to talk about Chapter 4 on Tuesday, then you should read Chapter 4 prior to coming to class on Tuesday. It is best to read it as close in time to class as possible. Previewing helps you learn more about the material to be discussed. You also have some idea about the main points before class. In this way you are able to predict the main points.

Previewing also lets you know how closely the teacher follows the textbook. If the teacher is following the book closely, then you can adjust your note-taking accordingly. You know that you can find the information in the book even if you miss something in class. You should regularly review your notes and make any connections between the class sessions. Some teachers forget where they leave off and end up repeating themselves. This can cause confusion among students. You should try to determine how organized your teachers are in their lectures.

By getting into the habit of previewing, you will enter class on a similar "wavelength" with the teacher. This will allow you to follow and participate in discussions. You will ask more intelligent questions and make pertinent comments about the subject. Previewing prepares your mind to receive and process the information. You will be learning the material gradually rather than waiting until the end of the term. If you gain at least a partial understanding of the material during previewing, then you can devote your time in lectures to determining and writing the main points.

Balance listening and writing

In order to keep up with the teacher's pace of talking, you need to develop a **BALANCE** between what you hear and what you write. As you listen you should be able to write at the same time, without interfering with your continuous process of listening. This is one of the most difficult aspects of note-taking. It takes constant practice and a high level of concentration. As you write, you must continue to hear what is being said. By having an idea of what is important, you can learn to ignore certain things while getting the main points. Maintaining eye contact with the teacher while writing can assist you in this process.

Re-writing and re-organizing notes

When you write rapidly, there is a tendency to be sloppy. Therefore, it is often not enough to keep notes in their original form. You will learn more from your notes if you can read them easily. After practice you might be able to get them neat and organized when you write them in class. However, at first you will probably need to re-write and re-organize your notes after class. It is worth the time to do this, especially if you want to learn from your notes. The resulting "handwritten textbook" could actually be a more accurate summary of the main points than the required textbook.

This re-writing and re-organizing shouldn't occupy too much of your time. As you do it you should eliminate any material that seems to be unnecessary. For example, if the teacher repeated the same point three times, you could keep only one of them and indicate that it was repeated. Use your own system to indicate importance, special relationships, or likely test questions. This period of re-writing should further your mastery of the material. While you do it you should be actively thinking about the material. It is not merely an exercise of copying your notes.

Why is it worth your time to go through this process? The main reason is that because teachers write tests, they are likely to emphasize what they covered in class. If you can accurately determine what the teacher considers to be important, then you have already done considerable studying for the test. This entire process takes time and work. But it allows you to study on an ongoing basis rather than trying to learn everything at once. You have made the most of your time in the classroom. Your class notes are neat and organized, which makes them easier to study. Reading the textbook is even easier after you have mastered the material presented in class. It is important to understand the reasons for going through this process. It is *NOT* busy work, but an effective way to learn and remember. If you are going to take the time and effort to take notes, then you should be certain that those notes are useful to you.

Using abbreviations

In order to keep up with the speaking pace of teachers, you will need to develop a consistent system of **ABBREVIATIONS**. In this way, you will be able to take more complete notes. It is virtually impossible to maintain a sufficiently fast pace without using some abbreviations. This process involves shortening long words. In addition, you should learn to eliminate unnecessary words. For example, you can get the main points without including every verb and connecting word. It is extremely important that you are able to understand your abbreviations after class. They won't do you any good if you forgot the meaning of the words or phrases.

If you can print faster than you can write, then do so. The main advantage of printing is that it tends to be easier to read. Use whatever method that works for you. If you miss something during a lecture, don't stop taking notes or give up. Just skip some space and find out what you missed after class or during a pause in the lectrue. Remember, you are supposed to be listening for **MAIN IDEAS**.

Examples

Let's assume that you are taking a class in Study Skills. This book is your textbook for that course. In this situation, you might use some of the following abbreviations during the lectures:

organization	– org.
note-taking	– n.t.
attention	– att. (don't confuse with *attitude*)
main points	– m.p.
previewing	– pre.
efficiency	– eff. (don't confuse with effectiveness)
study skills	– s.s.

Activity 6—Developing your own abbreviations

Based upon the material in this book, make a list of abbreviations that you would use during a lecture.

Word or phrase	Abbreviation

Listed below are some useful abbreviations:
1. Omit the words *a* and *the*.
2. Use these symbols:
   w/o — without
   vs. — versus
   = — equals
   & — and
   # — pound
   % — percent

3. Omit unnecessary periods and other punctuation.
4. Use only the first syllable such as:
   col – colony
   dem – democracy
   ach – achievement
5. Omit unnecessary vowels in words, like:
   backgd – background
   pkgd – packaged
   amt – amount
   rcd – received
6. Use apostrophes to shorten words
   am't – amount
   gov't – government
7. Use g for ing, as in:
   walkg – walking
   rung – running

The use of abbreviations is a personal matter. Don't copy another person's abbreviations unless you will remember their meaning. As you practice note-taking, you will develop your own system of abbreviations. Make it fun for yourself. It is often the most unusual or most personal material that is remembered. Eventually your abbreviations will become like second nature for you, and you will use them automatically.

The Cornell method of note-taking

There is a special method of taking notes that might be useful to you. Developed at Cornell University, it is called the Cornell method. To use this method, begin by making a vertical line on a piece of paper two and one-half inches from the left edge. You should use "loose leaf" paper rather than a spiral notebook. With the page properly divided (see diagram), you use the right side for taking notes in class. Follow the principles of note-taking discussed in this chapter. Close your eyes and see how many of those principles you can recall. Recite them aloud. The right side, labeled **RECORD**, should be used to write down the main ideas presented by the teacher. Write on one side of the page only.

As soon as possible after class, use the left side to **REDUCE** the notes you have taken into fewer words. This should be a summary of the ideas. Be careful not to *over*simplify, because that could distort the meaning. This reducing should not take too much time. Some material is presented in a form that is already condensed. Formulas cannot usually be reduced any further than they are; they come in reduced form.

The next step in this method is to cover the **RECORD** column with a piece of paper and attempt to **RECITE** an explanation of the words in the **REDUCE** column. In other words, you are expanding what was reduced. If you have any difficulty during this **RECITE** step, refer to the **RECORD** column for assistance. This reciting assists in the learning and memory of the material. You test yourself on a regular basis. You learn as the term progresses rather than waiting for the test.

After testing yourself, it is time to **REFLECT** (think about) the material. How does it relate to anything that you already know? What meaning or effect does it have on your life? Record any of your thoughts or opinions at this time.

The final step is **REVIEW**. This should be done on a regular basis. The more often that you review, the easier it will be for your test preparation. Regular review strengthens memory.

In sum, the major steps in the Cornell method of note-taking are:

1. Record   4. Reflect
2. Reduce   5. Review
3. Recite

Example

REDUCE	RECORD
Organization	Org cent to learng & mem to learn w/ more eff, we need to be org — both pers & w/ mat *****org v. imp to ss

The Cornell method uses some major principles of learning. It could also be used to take reading notes. You might want to only use part of the Cornell method. Another step, called **REACT**, could be added. At this time you could make any comments or state your opinions. This method is an example of the **ACTIVE LEARNING** discussed in Chapter 1. The more different ways that you experience information, the easier it will be for you to learn and remember it. There is another way to look at all of this information about listening and note-taking. The better you are at learning from lectures, the less you will have to depend upon your textbooks as a source of information. All of these processes are related to one another.

CHAPTER SUMMARY

1. The more that you learn and remember in class, the less work you will have outside of class.
2. The basic skills of attention and listening should be improved in order to take good notes.
3. The main thing about note-taking is to get the main points.
4. Previewing will help you to determine the main points and learn more during lectures.
5. You need to balance listening and writing in order to take notes effectively.
6. It is a good practice to re-write and re-organize your class notes in order to gain the full benefit from them.
7. Abbreviations assist you in keeping up with the pace of lectures.
8. The Cornell method of note-taking lets you learn as you go along. It consists of recording, reducing, reciting, reflecting, and reviewing.
9. Note-taking is one of the most important academic skills that you can develop. It will improve with practice.
10. Note-taking is not a substitute for listening.

CHAPTER 3

MEMORY: AN ESSENTIAL ACADEMIC AND LIFE SKILL

Overview

Memory is one of the most important skills that people need in order to be successful. Names, phone numbers, facts, directions, and procedures must be remembered if you are to make it through life without constantly referring to notes or books. There are easy and difficult ways to remember things; this chapter will show you the easy ways.

You should pay attention if you want to remember something. It helps to have the expressed intention of remembering certain information. Understanding should come before attempts to remember things. Structure and organization are essential to memory. There are a variety of mnemonic devices that allow you to remember things easier. It is important for you to determine exactly how you are supposed to remember material. You can save yourself much effort by using what you already know to memorize new material. You should use as many senses as possible in memorizing. Memory, like note-taking, is a personal process which you should develop with pride and care.

Basic conditions for memory

In order to remember something easily, you should have the **intention** of remembering it. You will remember certain things because of their sheer dramatic impact. For example, I still remember exactly what I was doing when I heard of President John F. Kennedy's assasination on November 22, 1963. I was in tenth grade at Pasadena High School, in a Representative Council meeting. The principal walked in unannounced, and told the group that President Kennedy had been shot and killed. My memory of other historical events is less vivid. We tend to forget most of the details soon after events occur.

For example, can you recall at this moment the names of everyone in all of your classes? Probably not, unless the class is small or if the teacher constantly repeats the name of each student. Besides, you don't have any reason to learn every name.

ATTENTION is another important component of memory. You should pay careful attention to information you wish to remember. **CONCENTRATION** is necessary if you want to remember things. People who are good at remembering names usually concentrate when they are introduced to others.

Activity 7 — What do you notice?

When you meet people, what is the first thing you usually notice about them?

It is much easier to remember something that you **UNDER-STAND** than something you don't understand. Some students try to memorize things before they understand them. This is a waste of effort. If you understand material **IN YOUR OWN WORDS** first, then memory will occur with less effort. For example, if you understand the elements of a chemical formula, you will remember it easier than if you try to memorize the symbols prior to understanding their meaning. Don't be in so much of a hurry to memorize that you neglect to reach an understanding of something.

The importance of structure and organization

One of the most common mistakes made by students is to try to memorize material that is disorganized. **ORGANIZATION** is central to memory. You will save yourself hours of frustration by finding the structure in information before attempting to memorize it. This applies to any subject. You can think of your memory as a kind of "computer". In this system, information must be "filed" in an orderly fashion so that you can retrieve it after it has been stored in your memory. Some information is presented in an organized manner. This makes it easier to remember. In other cases it will be your job to organize material so that you can memorize it easier.

Suppose you want to memorize the names of various athletic teams. You could first divide them into different sports such as basketball, baseball, and football. This **GROUPING** will assist your memory by triggering names within a category. This represents one type of organization. There are many others, depending upon the type of material to be memorized. For example, information could be organized by: theories, time periods, region, size, or type.

When trying to recall names, we might think of the category or role of the person, such as: fellow worker, fellow student, neighbor, parent, church member, friend, or teammate. In fact, when we forget things we can often recall them by finding their appropriate category. For example, you see someone whom you know to be familiar. However, you have difficulty remembering where you know the person from. You are stuck until you figure out the person is a clerk at the local market. Father Donovan is well known and remembered with his Roman collar. But when you see him at the beach, you temporarily forget his name. In other words, you have come to associate him so much with his role and religious clothing that you don't recognize him without it. Once you determine his category, then his name comes easily.

Some categories are already established, like the different subjects in school. You learn certain things in English, others in math, and others in history. There are cases when you need to organize material into groups before memorizing it. Let's say you had an assignment to memorize all of the states and state capitols. How would you approach the task? Would you think of the states in terms of geographical location, alphabetical order, or something else? Material will be much easier to memorize if you have it properly organized.

Activity 8 — Using categories to assist memory

Below you will find a list of words. First try to memorize the list in order. Then organize the words into groups and try to memorize them. Which list of words was easier to remember?

peanut	yellow
apple	walnut
pecan	grape
banana	macadamia
almond	avocado
cashew	green
red	purple

Condensing for storage and recall

There is a limit to the amount of material that our memories can hold at one time. Because of this, we should try to reduce the quantity of information to be memorized. The Cornell method (see Chapter 2) involves the process of reducing material. By reducing material, we actually memorize less and remember more. The important thing is to be able to expand the information that we have reduced. If a word represents a concept, then we should be able to explain that concept after we have pulled it out of our memory.

Example

Look at the following words. After reading each one of them, **RECITE** everything that you can remember about the word.

previewing

organization

efficiency

attitude

concentration

note-taking

memory

attention

Using all of your senses

Memory is aided by other factors. It is easier to remember things that we have experienced with most or all of our senses. For example, a foreign language is learned more quickly when we can see, hear, and speak it on a daily basis. Few become fluent in a language by only reading it. It is well documented that people learn a foreign language quicker and better when they live in the native land of that language.

Suppose you have never smelled a skunk. Your only knowledge of skunks has come from books. In this situation, what might you imagine the smell of a skunk would be like? It could involve a variety of familiar smells. However, once you have smelled a skunk it is quite likely you will never forget that distinctive odor. The same is true of garlic, baking bread, or exhaust fumes.

In using our various senses, we gain a more complete knowledge of the material to be remembered. Writing and reciting are both examples of using different senses to assist memory. Using "flash cards" is another way to help you remember things. Perhaps the slowest and least efficient way to remember something is to merely read it over and over. It is far better to think about it, talk abut it, write it, keep it organized, reduce it, pay attention to it, concentrate on it, intend to remember it, smell it, touch it, and taste it (if possible).

Example

If you are learning to fix an automobile engine, your memory is important. You might want to first read something about how engines operate. However, reading is not enough to make you a mechanic. You need to practice fixing engines. You will remember how to repeat the process by paying attention to locations, sounds, and other factors that could never be learned from reading alone.

Activity 9—Testing your memory

What do you remember about memory? Write everything you can recall below. After you have done that, then briefly go back and look over this chapter to see what you forgot. Did you remember things better if they were mentioned in previous chapters?

Regular review

Another thing that aids memory is **REGULAR REVIEW**. A short period of time spent in review each day is worth more than longer periods of cramming. Cramming to pass tests is not necessary if you review on a regular basis. Think about how you learned the phone numbers of people that you call often. By regular review you continually strengthen the weaker aspects of your memory. Those are the things you tend to forget. Focus more attention on the material that you forget.

It is quite valuable to review the previous lesson or chapter before moving on to the next one. By doing this you prevent the normal process of forgetting. For example, people who are good at remembering names often repeat a person's name in the course of their conversation. "I understand your point of view, Frank."

The use of associations and mental images

We all have a past history which either assists or impairs our ability to memorize. When we learn something, we often use **ASSOCIATIONS** with familiar material to assist us. These associations might trigger our memory by reminding us of something that we already know. For example, if you have an aunt named Lila who wears gaudy clothes, you might think of Aunt Lila when you meet other women who wear gaudy clothes. Or else you might think of her if you meet someone named Lila.

You can make use of any past knowledge, experience, or interest that assists you in remembering things. I have a friend who memorizes phone numbers by relating them to the numbers of certain athletes. This works well for him, because he is an expert on sports. His system wouldn't work for someone who did not know much about sports. What past knowledge do you use to assist you in learning and remembering new material?

In some cases you can use **MENTAL IMAGES** to enhance your memory. When you meet Mr. Urban Hunter, you might imagine a man hunting animals in the city. Owen Spann, a talk show host on KGO radio in San Francisco, could be remembered by the images of owing a bridge toll (Owen) on the Golden Gate span (Spann). If an appropriate image can be applied, then it should be used. However, it is sometimes a waste of time to invent images which are likely to be forgotten. Take advantage of your past, unusual material, and your imagination to improve your memory.

Verbatim memory vs. remembering the idea

It is important to determine whether you are supposed to learn material word for word or merely to remember the basic idea or concept. The two types of memory are different, and you need to be certain of which type of memory is appropriate in various situations. It is a waste of effort to memorize something verbatim that only needs to be understood in general terms. On the other hand, you should memorize languages and quotations verbatim. What other types of material should be memorized verbatim?

Mnemonic devices

There are a variety of so-called **MNEMONIC DEVICES** which can be used to improve memory. These devices allow you to simplify information and to use certain tricks to remember things. The major mnemonic devices are as follows:

1. *Rhyme*

Rhymes provide us with clues about information. Songs can be remembered partially because of certain rhyming patterns. Instead of learning how to spell every word that has an i and e together, you can use the following rhyme: "I before E except after C, or when sounded like A as in neighbor and weigh." There are other exceptions to this rule. Most of them are included in this sentence: "The leisured foreigners neither seized either species nor forfeited their weird heights." Another example is the ABC's as they are learned by young children. It is unlikely that they would learn the alphabet as easily if they didn't use the rhyming pattern. Sometimes you can create rhymes when they don't occur naturally.

2. *Rhythm*

The method of rhythm is used commonly in songs, prayers, poems, and spelling. It is also part of the reason that the ABC's are learned. Rhythm assists us in memorizing such things as phone numbers, Social Security numbers, and addresses. Try to remember the following phone numbers: 6857-395, 7854-980, and 4536-685. You are probably so accustomed to seeing three numbers first (685-7395, 785-4980, and 453-6685) that it is hard to even consider them to be phone numbers unless they fit a certain rhythm pattern. **RHYTHM** is a difficult word to spell. However, it is much easier if you break it up like this: rhy thm and say it in a rhythmic pattern. Try to notice how you use rhythm to memorize new information.

3. *Acronyms*

This device makes use of the first letter of words to trigger our memory. For example, the acronym **HOMES** can help us remember the Great Lakes: Huron, Ontario, Michigan, Erie, and Superior. The name Roy G. Biv represents the colors of the visual spectrum: red, orange, yellow, green, blue, indigo, and violet. Some acronyms occur naturally, while others must be invented. Some of the more famous ones are: IRS, NASA, USA, VIP, and CIA. Can you think of any others? If so, write them in the space below.

4. *Sentences*

You can use sentences to represent certain ideas or words. For example, if you wanted to remember the notes of the musical scale, you need only remember the sentence: Every Good Boy Does Fine. The Great Lakes could be remembered by this sentence: See My Horse Eat Oats. Which method do you find easier to remember the Great Lakes, acronyms or sentence?

5. *Location*

Location can provide important clues about information. Teachers learn their students' names partially because of the seating chart. It would be more difficult for them to learn the names if the students sat in a different seat every day. The method of location can be used in remembering directions or the state capitols. The ancient Greek orators used location in order to remember their speeches. They would make associations between certain objects and ideas. Then all they needed to do was recall the objects. That would then trigger the memory of the connected concepts. When we lose something, it is often location that assists us in eventually finding it. We recall when and where we last remember having the object, and gradually trace its location.

6. *Link method*

This technique involves connecting items which need to be memorized in order. It is done by making unusual links among the successive items. These connections are made into a story. If the story can be recalled, then the words will be also.

7. *Examples*

The use of examples or illustrations is one of the best ways to remember things. The examples can be as unusual as you want, as long as they assist in memory.

Memory is a very personal thing. What works for one person might have no meaning for someone else. Some people are more visually-oriented in their memory, while others favor sounds or feelings. Do you need to see things in order to remember them? Think about your memory. What techniques suggested in this chapter will you be able to use? How does a waitress remember an order, a bus driver a route, or a cook a recipe? How much do you remember about memory?

Activity 10 — Using the link method

Make up a story, using unusual and bizarre connections, with the following words:

dog

ashtray

paper

plant

fence

car

egg

suitcase

phone

shoe

light

CHAPTER SUMMARY

1. Memory is an essential academic and life skill, which can be improved with practice and certain methods.
2. Intention, attention, and understanding are all necessary for effective memory.
3. In order to memorize well, it is useful to have the material organized.
4. Grouping assists the memory process.
5. Condensing material aids memory by reducing the amount of material to be memorized.
6. The more senses you use, the easier it will be to remember things.
7. Material should be reviewed regularly to prevent forgetting.
8. Associations and mental images enable you to use your experience to help you memorize material.
9. You should determine whether you need to memorize material word for word or merely understand the concept.
10. Mnemonic devices provide various tricks and shortcuts. They include: rhyme, rhythm, acronyms, sentences, location, the link method, and examples.

Notes

CHAPTER 4

TIME-MANAGEMENT

Overview

One of the chief attributes of a good student is the ability to make the maximum use of time. Time-management styles vary from person to person, and should be selected on a realistic basis. There is little use in setting up a schedule that you will ignore. By making a time chart you will be able to determine exactly how you are spending your time currently. It is useful to examine your priorities, and plan your time according to what is most important for you. You should become more aware of your typically most productive times, and try to get your most important work done during that period.

How do you work? Your work patterns can be considered when you plan your use of time. The length of study periods will vary depending upon many factors. Some people are more rigid than others in their daily schedules. You might have a personal ritual that helps prepare you to perform a certain task. Master calendars provide you with a long-range listing of what you have to do. They should be in a central location, and all important dates should be listed. The calendars should be consulted regularly. It is your time, and if you use it wisely you will have more of it for yourself.

Making a time chart: examining your priorities

The first step in learning to manage your time more efficiently is to make a time chart, which assesses your current use and waste of time. Try to determine exactly how you are spending your time in a typical week. Make sure to distinguish between **FIXED** and **FLEXIBLE** activities. Class is an example of a fixed activity, occurring at the same time each day (or several times a week). Recreation might be a flexible activity, taking place at various times during the week. By making a time chart you will begin to get a better sense about your **PRIORITIES**. For example, if you spend twenty hours a week watching televison, that should tell you something about your priorities.

Where does school fit into your life? Before you answer this question, think carefully about it. Your answer will largely determine how much time and effort you spend on studying. If you consider school to be a high priority, then you should allot enough time to complete your work.

Activity 11 — Ranking your priorities

Rank in order the ten most important things in your life.

1.   6.

2.   7.

3.   8.

4.   9.

5.   10.

In order to succeed in school, you need enough time to finish your assignments, study for tests, and think about the subjects that you are taking. Do not expect to do well in school if you do not spend enough time studying. It takes time to learn things. Some people can learn them faster and better than others. People are not always ready to study when they are supposed to study. For this reason, it is better to allow a few extra hours for mood changes, warm-up, and distractions.

Activity 12 — Making a time chart

On the next page you will find a Daily Activity Schedule. As soon as possible, chart your activities hour by hour for one full week. Be honest. Your are only fooling yourself if you say you study more than you actually do. This charting will take time and will make you more aware of how you are currently spending your time. It is best to do this time chart on a "typical" week. You could do it for more than one week if you want.

After making your time chart, ask yourself the following questions:
1. Am I wasting time?
2. Am I spending enough time to complete my studying?
3. Does my time use reflect my priorities?
4. How can I change my current use of time?
5. Am I trying to do too many things at once?

DAILY ACTIVITY SCHEDULE

Name _____   Date _____

Time	Monday	Tuesday	Wednesday	Thursday	Friday	Saturday	Sunday	Time
06:00 06:30								06:00 06:30
07:00 07:30								07:00 07:30
08:00 08:30								08:00 08:30
09:00 09:30								09:00 09:30
10:00 10:30								10:00 10:30
11:00 11:30								11:00 11:30
12:00 12:30								12:00 12:30
01:00 01:30								01:00 01:30
02:00 02:30								02:00 02:30
03:00 03:30								03:00 03:30
04:00 04:30								04:00 04:30
05:00 05:30								05:00 05:30
06:00 06:30								06:00 06:30
07:00 07:30								07:00 07:30
08:00 08:30								08:00 08:30
09:00 09:30								09:00 09:30
10:00 10:30								10:00 10:30

Your typical "body time"

What is your best time for studying? Some people are alert and full of energy when they first awake. Others take more time to get going in the morning. We each tend to be more alert during certain times of the day. It is best to get your most important or difficult work done during your best times of day. The next time you find yourself studying well, examine the time and see if there is any consistency to when you are most productive. Make an effort to accomplish as much as you can during that period. However, don't use "body time" as an excuse for not studying at other times. Typical performance does not mean that you are limited to performing at certain hours.

Activity 13 — Assessing your typical work patterns

Write down a brief description of how you work. Are you slow or fast? Do you skip from task to task? Do you work for long periods without taking a break?

Length of study periods

One way to make better use of time is to use short periods during the day that you usually waste. Riding on the bus, between classes, before meals, and other odd times can be used effectively for studying. You might use these short time periods to make lists of priorities that you can complete when you have more time. This time could also be used to do short assignments, plan your time, and to think about school. You would be surprised at how much you can accomplish in a short period of time if you are concentrating properly.

Working effectively also involves the ability to take and fully enjoy breaks. Use breaks as a reward for completing something or after a productive study period. Exercise, listen to music, have something to eat, or do whatever is relaxing or invigorating for you. Sometimes you need to think about something totally different from school during breaks. At other times your breaks can be used to reflect about your subjects. The timing of breaks is important. You should be careful not to let breaks interfere with your momentum.

The exact period that you study at one time will vary depending upon several factors. Some subjects are more difficult to spend long periods of time on than others. If you get very involved in a task, don't feel that you must take a break at a specific time. That might disrupt your momentum and concentration. Sometimes you will be able to work on one task for hours without losing your effectiveness. When it does happen, be careful not to break up the "groove." Use your level of productivity as a guide in deciding the length of your study periods. Too many breaks can cause you to spend unnecessary time on a task. Not enough breaks can also prevent you from working to your potential.

Momentum: the order of studying various subjects

It is important to choose an effective order for studying your subjects. Here is a general suggestion. Begin with activities that tend to get you warmed up properly. Don't always save the most difficult subjects for last. If you do, you might end up being too tired to be effective. Find a pattern that allows you to concentrate fully on each subject. Vary the order depending upon the specific assignments, due dates, or upcoming tests. It is often useful to be considerably warmed up prior to beginning a writing assignment, due to the amount of creativity needed.

The exact order that you select should be based upon the time of day, specific needs, possible mood variations, and an analysis of your successes. If you find something that works for you, repeat it.

Planning time realistically

At the beginning of this chapter I mentioned the importance of selecting a time schedule that is realistic for you. Think once again about what kind of person you are. You should be getting good at that by now. Which aspects of your personality seem to be fairly stable or permanent? What parts are more like **HABITS** which could be changed? Be careful not to set up a schedule that you would only adhere to for a short period of time.

Successful use of time involves knowing when **NOT** to study as well as when to study. If there is an unusual amount of excitement because of a special event, if might be better to join in the fun than to sit in front of your books for hours and daydream about the event. You need to learn when certain conditions make effective studying almost impossible. Remember, you are rewarded on the basis of **RESULTS** rather than the amount of time spent studying.

Rituals

We all have certain rituals that we go through before doing things. Your ritual for studying might involve cleaning off your desk, getting a drink, taking a shower, or changing your clothes. Rituals are natural and acceptable, as long as they don't occupy too much time and energy. If a certain ritual helps you to prepare yourself for studying, use it. But be honest with yourself. Don't use the ritual to stall the process of studying.

I have my own rituals when I write. Most of them are not really necessary, but they help me get mentally prepared to write. I always like to have something to drink, a fresh piece of correction tape, and a clean desk. I do not write as well if there are pressing thoughts on my mind.

Activity 14 — Examining your use of rituals

What rituals do you use in studying or preparing to study? Do they help you or actually delay the completion of tasks? Do you use any effective rituals in other aspects of your life that could be applied in some way to studying?

Making and keeping schedules

A major part of effective time-management is to keep an up-to-date schedule of dates and activities. This includes maintaining a **MASTER CALENDAR** which lists all test dates, holidays, and due dates for long term assignments. By having a master calendar, you will always be aware of upcoming events. Don't rely on remembering to look at your course outline, because you don't always have it in front of you.

By now you should have some idea of what kind of schedule will work for you. Are your classes bunched too close together? Do you have enough time to devote to each class? A schedule is merely a **GUIDE**. Be willing to revise it in response to changing conditions.

Developing habits of productive studying

Perhaps the key to effective time-management is **ORGANIZATION**. You will save yourself countless hours by organizing your work area. Think about how much time you waste looking for lost items such as books, notebooks, pens, or papers. Take the time to organize **YOUR STUDY AREA** so that you will know where to find things when you need them. Check from time to time to see if you are satisfied with the way things are organized. Develop your own **SYSTEM** that makes sense to you.

Time-management does not mean that you have to be regimented. It simply means that you waste little time and become aware of how you are using time. You need to become aware of both your short-term and long-term goals. Time conflicts are often the result of differences between these two types of goals. People often procrastinate because they are unable to break down a task into components. Make a start, and the rest of the task will be completed later. The better you manage your time, the more free time you will have to do what you want. I'd like to keep talking about this, but I'm running out of time. Aren't we all?

CHAPTER SUMMARY

1. One of the first steps in learning to manage your
   make a time chart.
2. By examining your priorities you will be able to pla
   time better.
3. You should attempt to become aware of your typical "be
   time" and work patterns.
4. The length of study periods will vary depending upon
   interest, time of day, momentum, and the subject matter.
5. When setting up a schedule, it is important to be realistic.
6. Personal rituals have their place, but can be abused if
   carried to extremes and used to avoid studying.
7. It is useful to have a master calendar which includes all
   important dates in one central location.
8. Organization is important in time-management.
9. Time-management styles should be selected on the basis of
   self-awareness.
10. Procrastination is often the result of not being able to
    break a large task into component parts.

CHAPTER 5

HOW TO READ EFFICIENTLY

Overview

Reading takes more time than any single activity associated with studying. You need to read effectively if you are going to succeed in school. There are many different kinds of reading assignments: scientific, literature, math, and current events to name a few. Your style and purpose of reading will be different in these various cases.

Reading demands a high level of concentration. An active approach to reading (thinking, writing, reciting) tends to raise your level of concentration. It is very important to develop your vocabulary, as words are the building blocks of reading material. Sometimes it is useful to find different books on the same subject in order to increase your interest and understanding of certain material.

You should be aware of the different parts of books such as the glossary, index, table of contents, and appendix. Certain material is contained in those sections rather than in the body of the text. Mental intensity can be increased by using your finger as a pacer, skimming, and scanning.

Different kinds of reading assignments

The way in which you read something depends upon the purpose of a particular assignment. Are you reading for general meaning, verbatim memory, or basic theme? The pace of reading should be adjusted to the type of material. For example, you might read a short story more quickly than an explanation of how to perform a math problem. Before you begin to read something, try to determine what kind of material it is and how you should approach the reading assignment.

You should also decide how many times you plan to read something. This will depend in part upon the amount of time you have available. For example, if you are only going to read something once, then you should attempt to remember what you are reading as you go along. If you have more time to spend, then the first reading might be more leisurely.

Basic principles of reading

I have been emphasizing the principles of alertness, attentiveness, and active learning throughout the book. The same principles apply to any kind of reading. If you want to understand and remember what you read, assume a physical position that allows you to be as alert as possible. Although you might enjoy the comfort of an easy chair, couch, or bed, those forms of relaxation are not suited for absorbing written material.

Reading demands a higher level of concentration than most other activities. If you have other things on your mind or if you are restless, it is probably not the best time for reading. You should do reading assignments at times when you can direct your full attention on them. If you are not in the mood to read but want to accomplish some school-related task, then do something else. Successful students are able to determine the best time to perform various tasks.

Suggestions for increasing concentration: active reading

To keep yourself alert and focused on the reading material, it helps to take some kind of notes. If you can write in the book, underlining or some other form of marking main ideas can be done. The main purpose of underlining is to make a note of the **MAIN POINTS**. You can easily find them during a second reading or review. You can also develop your own system of notations which direct you to the main points.

If you aren't allowed to write in the book, you can take notes on separate paper. The same principles apply to that. You can also write down reactions, comments, or questions about the material. This note-taking should not interfere with the flow or pace of your reading. You should be trying to relate the reading to what you already know.

Do not become discouraged if you don't understand or remember material after reading it only once. It often takes two or three readings (and a lecture) before you will grasp something. Your reading should be connected with lectures and discussions in order to improve learning. The more you can relate and combine the various sources of information, the better off you will be. Previewing helps you understand the lecture, and the lecture helps you understand the material in the book.

There are times when you will absorb much of the material that you are reading. When this happens, make note of the surrounding conditions. What time of day is it, what kind of lighting do you have, and so forth? When you are unable to focus and concentrate, it is sometimes better to take a break and change some of the conditions. Continue to **EXPERIMENT** with your reading until you discover a successful formula.

Developing your vocabulary

One of the major difficulties that students face in reading is weakness in vocabulary. You are not going to be able to read easily if you have difficulty understanding many of the words. It is essential for you to continually increase your vocabulary. In fact, you will save yourself many hours by devoting at least an hour per week to improving your vocabulary. There are books available on this subject. In addition, you should keep a dictionary handy to look up difficult words.

You need to know the difference between a dictionary definition of a word and a definition which might be used in a specific subject. For example, consider the word reinforcement. It means one thing to a carpenter, another to an Army general, and yet another to a psychologist. There are many other examples of these subject-specific definitions. Use the **GLOSSARY** of books to find the specialized meanings of words. You cannot continue to ignore your deficiencies in vocabulary. Words are the building blocks of education. If you don't improve your **VOCABULARY AND SPELLING**, then you won't achieve academic excellence. This becomes increasingly important as you advance through school.

Using alternate sources

One of the most common complaints made by students is that their books are either too difficult or too boring. This may or may not actually be true. But if it is, I will offer a suggestion. Try another source on the same subject. Go to the library or bookstore and find a book that is more interesting or that explains things better. After reading the alternate source, try to read the assigned textbook. It should have more meaning at that point. Make sure that you know what is contained in the required book, because the test questions will be taken from that source. The alternate book can be used to explain ideas or to arouse your interest. Books have different ways of explaining information. You should make note of such differences.

Increasing mental intensity

Try to develop increased **INTENSITY** while you read. This might involve reading at a faster pace or thinking about what you are reading. Use your finger as a pacer to increase reading speed. Develop mental pictures while you read. Don't just read the words. Develop your own examples which will help you understand and remember the material. Test yourself from time to time to see if you are able to remember what you have read. Remember, **LEARNING IS AN ACTIVE PROCESS**. Think about what the instructor has said in class and how it relates to what you are reading.

The different parts of books

There are ways to read other than reading from the front to back cover. You should get into the habit of **SURVEYING** a book before reading it. Every book is a bit different. You should learn about the format, style, and parts of each book you read. Does the book have a glossary, index, chapter summaries, overview, questions, or appendix? Is there a separate index for information and people? The preface and introduction tell you something about the author and purpose of the book. It might also tell you something important about the perspective of the author. Don't be in a hurry to get to Chapter 1. A bit of preparation will help get you oriented to the book. This will make reading it easier and more enjoyable.

Skimming and scanning

Try skimming the entire book before reading it. Are there illustrations, diagrams, or italics? Does the author use **BOLD-FACE PRINT** to emphasize the main ideas? Chapter summaries are useful in determining the main ideas. They can even be read before reading the chapter in order to alert you to the main ideas. Questions at the end of the chapter provide you with valuable clues about what you should be focusing on while reading. In some cases you will want to scan for certain information rather than reading an entire section.

In some cases you will be assigned more than one book in a course. Then you can study material topic by topic rather than chapter by chapter. There are many different ways that you can approach reading other than the conventional ones. You should review what you read on a regular basis to aid in the retention of material.

CHAPTER SUMMARY

1. You need to learn how to read effectively if you want to be successful in school.
2. There are different kinds of reading assignments, and different reading styles associated with each of them.
3. Reading demands a high level of alertness and concentration.
4. By taking an active approach to reading, concentration is increased. This involves writing and taking notes as well as thinking.
5. It is important to develop your vocabulary.
6. If your required textbook is too difficult or boring, it is wise to select an alternate source to help you learn the material.
7. Increasing mental intensity can be accomplished by using your finger as a pacer, testing yourself, or thinking about your reading.
8. As a student you should be aware of the different parts of books such as the index, glossary, preface, and appendix.
9. Skimming and scanning can be used in addition to studying material topic by topic.
10. There are many different ways that you can approach reading other than the conventional ways.

Notes

CHAPTER 6

PREPARING FOR AND TAKING TESTS

Overview

This chapter discusses both test-preparation and test-taking. There is really no substitute for knowing the material. However, that alone is not enough to get you through all tests. Tests are not always fair or clearly written. But as a student you need to learn to deal effectively in a test-taking situation.

There is no substitute for regular review. Cramming is less effective than studying on a regular basis. In addition to knowing the material, you should learn to anticipate the questions as you study. You should also write answers to those questions. A positive, confident state of mind is very helpful in preparing for and taking tests.

Once you get into the test-taking situation, you should survey the test and plan your time. Read the directions and test questions very carefully. If you have any questions, ask the teacher. Answer the easy questions first. This will increase your confidence, give you more points, and assist you in answering the more difficult items. Answer every question unless there is a penalty for guessing. Proofread your answers after you are done. Try to learn from previous tests.

Regular review: the basis of test preparation

One principle of learning emphasized throughout this book is to **STUDY ON A REGULAR BASIS**. The more times and different ways that you experience material, the easier it is to learn and remember. When you study regularly, studying for tests is simply a matter of review. It is much easier to learn information bit by bit than to "cram" for tests in a short period of time. When you cram you take a risk that your mind will be working properly on a certain day or night. If it does, then you might be able to pass the test. However, things do not always go so smoothly. Another problem with cramming is fatigue. Your mind won't be as alert during the test if you burn your energy during the cramming session.

When you study regularly you are better able to organize the information properly. You can think about the various relationships. Perhaps the only advantage of cramming is that you finally feel enough pressure to study and remember things. But this is greatly outweighed by the many disadvantages.

Emphasize key ideas

When studying for a test, you need to spend more time on certain areas than others. The **KEY IDEAS** should be given more attention than the trivial or less important ideas. If you **PAY ATTENTION** you should have a good idea about what is important.

Activity 15 — Finding main ideas in this book

Let's pretend that you have to prepare for a test on this book. Based upon **REPETITION, BOLDFACE PRINT, AND EMPHASIS,** what are the main ideas in this book? Make a list of them below in as few words as possible. Then try to expand upon them through conversation and writing.

Anticipate test questions

One of the major aspects of effective test preparation is to anticipate test questions. There are several ways that you can do this:

1. Look at previous tests given by the instructor.
2. Look at the questions (if any) in the textbook.
3. Make up probable questions based upon the main ideas.

Whatever you do between the first and last day of class, you should attempt to **PREDICT** exactly what questions will be asked on the tests. In addition to predicting the questions, you should write **AND** recite answers to the questions. Based upon what you have learned thus far in this book, why should you do this? Sometimes the teacher will even give you the questions prior to the test.

Your ability to take a test depends upon how accurately you predict the questions. You also need to have accurate and complete answers to those questions. Many students know the material well enough. However, they haven't bothered to consider the types of questions that could be asked about the material. A test is a way of transforming information in various ways into different forms of questions. For example, the California written driving test is a group of multiple-choice questions that have been taken from the handbook. Test questions might come as a surprise to you if you don't anticipate the questions. Be careful not to assume that you have accurately predicted the questions. In other words, play it safe by studying the material thoroughly.

Activity 16—Writing a list of questions from this book

Based upon the information in this book, make a list of questions in the following formats: true-false, multiple-choice, fill-in, and essay. Then develop answers for those questions.

True-False

1.

2.

3.

4.

5.

Multiple-Choice

1.

2.

3.

4.

5.

Fill-In

1.

2.

3.

4.

5.

Essay

1.

2.

3.

4.

5.

Before the test: the proper mental attitude

Before moving into the actual test-taking situation, let's consider some things about your thoughts and behavior prior to the test. You should be rested and as comfortable as possible. You should be relaxed, but not overly so. A little bit of tension can provide you with additional motivation. Don't go into a test when you are hungry, thirsty, or having to go to the bathroom. Take care of those matters before entering the classroom. ***YOU SHOULD MAKE EVERY EFFORT TO BE AT YOUR BEST*** when you take a test. You should use any rituals that help get you mentally prepared for a test.

There is usually no need to go over your notes frantically prior to a test. It might be useful to review some **KEY WORDS**. But that depends upon your level of mastery. You will not raise your score much by last second cramming. **CONFI-DENCE** is a crucial factor in taking tests. You might weaken your confidence by such last minute sessions. Come to class ready to take the test with pens, pencils, paper, and whatever else you might need. You should bring a watch in order to budget your time. At a certain point you should reach a level of satisfaction and acceptance of your readiness. This is a critical point, whether you are at the A or C level. At that point, for better or worse, you are ready to take the test.

Read directions and questions carefully

When you receive the test, make sure and listen for any additional verbal instructions given by the teacher. Try not to let any source of external distraction interfere with your concentration. Your goal is to get as many items correct as you possibly can. In order to do so, you must **READ THE DIRECTIONS AND TEST QUESTIONS VERY CAREFULLY**.

There is no reason to miss any question because of careless-ness. Briefly **SURVEY** the entire test to get a feeling for it. At this point you should develop some general plan for budget-ing your time. How long can you afford to spend on each question if you want to complete the test? Are some items going to take longer than others? Is the teacher giving you enough time to finish the test? For example, if there are fifty objective questions and you have an hour to complete the test, you should allot approximately one minute per item. Of course, some items might take longer than others. In planning your time, you should not take too much time. Sometimes you can plan ahead if the teacher tells you how many questions are going to be on the test.

Taking the strain off your memory

Some of what you memorize is not very secure in your memory. If essay or fill-in questions demand that type of information, you should write down some **MEMORY DEVICES** (such as acronyms) before proceeding to other sections of the test. In this way you don't have to worry about forgetting that information. You have relieved your memory, and can then direct your full attenion on the other questions.

Points per item

If the test specifies the number of points per item, then you should select certain items over others. Be sure to notice which items are worth more points. You can determine this when you survey the test. For example, if essay questions are worth twenty-five points and matching questions are worth one point, then you should spend more time on the essay questions. Your basic aim is to get the maximum possible score on the test.

Answer the easy items first

Rather than going straight through the test in order, it is better to **ANSWER THE EASY QUESTIONS FIRST.** This will serve several important purposes. First of all, you will build up your confidence. Secondly, you will get more questions correct even if you run out of time. There is no reason to miss the easy questions due to lack of time or poor planning. You can make some type of notation by the items you skip for easy relocation. Another reason for answering the easy questions first is that it can assist you in answering the difficult items.

There are many times when certain test items will trigger your memory and assist you in answering other items. You should examine tests carefully for such clues. In addition, you should take as much time as you are allowed to give your memory the opportunity to work completely. You will not always remember everything at the beginning of a test. The more you work on it, certain facts will be recalled. You might think of a test as a kind of puzzle to solve. If you take enough time and try different approaches, then you can often answer questions that at first appeared too difficult. It is often the persistent student who is the most successful. Don't give up too easily.

Answer every item

What if you just don't know the answer to a question? Unless there is a "penalty for guessing" (a certain number of points subtracted for each wrong answer, as in the SAT), I recommend that you make an educated guess. You can do this by eliminating obviously incorrect answers. Research shows that guessing will get you a higher score even with guessing penalties. Look at it this way. There is no chance of getting an item correct if you leave it blank. If you make a "wild" guess it is not much better. So give it a try and you will have a better chance of increasing your total number of points. On true-false questions, you have about a 50% chance of getting items correct merely by guessing. It is to your advantage to guess especially in those cases.

Give the best answer

One of the most common reasons for missing items on tests is when you provide a good answer but not the **BEST** answer. In most cases the teacher is looking for the best possible answer. Therefore, it is important to look at all possible choices before making your final decision. Don't be too hasty. It may cause you valuable points and influence your grade. While you study you should anticipate questions that ask you to distinguish between a good and the best answer.

Proofread answers

After you have completed a test, you should make a **HABIT** of checking your work for mistakes. There is no reason to lose points because of mistakes that could be avoided. If you have a strong feeling to change an answer, then do so. However, be careful not to second-guess all of your original answers. **READ THE QUESTIONS CAREFULLY** for tricks, hidden meaning, the words *not, every, only, never,* and other words that can change the entire meaning of a question. Take as much time as you need to complete the test. Work at **YOUR OWN PACE**. Don't be influenced by the pace of others.

If a question is vague, ask the teacher about it. It is possible that the teacher made a mistake on the wording or assumed that students understood the meaning of a question. If a certain word or phrase prevents you from understanding a question, then ask for the meaning. The worst the teacher can do is to refuse to answer your question. However, there are some teachers who don't allow you to ask any questions. If so, try to do your best under the circumstances. Use your knowledge of the teacher to help you decide whether to ask a question or not. Common sense will take you a long way in these situations.

Learning from a test

After your test is graded and returned to you, look it over carefully to see what mistakes you made. Learn from your mistakes by finding out what you missed and why you missed it. The most common reasons for missing items are as follows:
1. Misreading the question.
2. Writing "around" the answer.
3. Carelessness.
4. Poor organization.
5. Incomplete answers.
6. Failing to give the best answer.
You should also find out what you got correct merely by

guessing. A test can provide you with valuable clues about the teacher and what you might expect on future tests from that teacher.

If teachers make mistakes in grading your papers, tell them about it in a tactful manner. Some teachers gain respect for students who are genuinely concerned about their answers and test scores. You should consider the following questions:

1. What kinds of items does the teacher include in the test?
2. Are the questions tricky or direct?
3. Does the teacher test on main ideas or trivia and details?
4. What clues or hints are provided by the teacher before and on the test?

By answering those questions, you will be better prepared for future tests. Learn the correct answer to each item, even if you missed it. Getting a test back should be used as a learning experience. You should be concerned with more than just the grade you received. Learn from both your mistakes and correct answers. Try not to repeat the same mistakes again.

Types of questions

There are various types of questions which commonly appear on tests. You should become familiar with each type of question. In this way you will be better prepared to take any test.

1. Multiple-Choice

This type of question demands that you select the **BEST** answer from several alternatives. Before looking at the choices, it is useful to try to complete the answer. You can do this by anticipating the answer by looking at the first part of the question. Then you can look at the choices. Make sure you read every possibility before making your decision. These questions can be especially difficult if you don't know the material thoroughly.

You can use a process of elimination in some cases. Start by eliminating choices which are obviously incorrect. After you have selected your answer, read the entire statement to make certain that it makes sense. If it doesn't, then try another choice. Multiple-choice questions often use such phrases as: all of the above, none of the above, and only a and c. Be aware of the various ways in which multiple-choice questions are worded. For example, the first choice is often a good answer but not the best answer to a question. Many students don't take the time to look at all of the choices before making their decision.

Examples

1. A method of note-taking which involves dividing the page is called:
   a. the Corvell method
   b. the Cornett method
   c. the Cornwall method
   d. none of the above

The correct answer is d. The first three choices are misspelled. You would have to know the spelling to get that item correct.

2. Which of the following is not a step in the Cornell method?
   a. reflect
   b. review
   c. reduce
   d. remake
   e. record

The correct answer is d. You would have to know each step to know which one does not fit. Some teachers would not underline the word not for you. That is why it is so important to **READ THE QUESTIONS CAREFULLY**.

3. Using the name Roy G. Biv to remember the colors is called:
   a. useless
   b. location
   c. an acronym
   d. the link method

The correct answer is c.

2. *True-false*

True-false questions demand extremely **CAREFUL READING**. One word can make the difference between a true and false statement. Be especially careful of words that indicate absolutes such as always, never, only, all, and none. These usually mean that the statements are false. Another common type of question is one in which one of two clauses is false. In those cases, the entire statement is false.

Examples

1. Of all recent Democratic Presidents, Nixon was the only one to resign. (This is false because Nixon is a Republican.)
2. Since he is the foremost authority on adults, Dr. Spock is considered an expert. (This is false because Dr. Spock is an expert on children.)
3. In reducing material, it is helpful to oversimplify. (This is false because of the *over*.)

3. *Matching*

Survey the choices before beginning to answer matching questions. Count them to see if there is an equal number on each side. Answer the easy items first. Try to keep your thinking flexible, as the connections are of various types. They can be definitions, explanations, or other relationships. Make sure your answers make sense after you complete them.

Examples

1. Cornell method	a. a way of taking notes
2. Organization	b. word for word
3. Verbatim	c. demand planning before writing
4. Essay questions	d. aids in memory
5. Reduce	e. condense

The correct answers are 1.–a., 2.–d., 3.–b., 4.–c., 5.–e.

4. *Essay questions*

Essay questions are more subject to the unique judgements of individual teachers than the previous types. It is important to become aware of a teacher's preferences and expectations. However, there are certain principles that apply to most situations.

First of all, read the question carefully and see exactly what is being asked. After determining the nature of the question, think about everything that you know related to it. Write down that information and a brief outline before writing. Don't take too long working on the outline. Once you have a basic structure, then begin to write. Always proofread your work after you are finished.

In general, students lose points on essay questions for the following reasons:

1. They fail to answer the question that is asked.
2. They do not provide sufficient examples or evidence to support their statements.
3. They either write too much or not enough. The best rule is to stay to the point and answer the question.
4. They are disorganized.
5. Their writing is sloppy.
6. They don't follow directions.
7. They don't use any transitions between paragraphs or ideas.

CHAPTER SUMMARY

1. There is no substitute for regular review.
2. When studying for a test, emphasize the main ideas.
3. It is helpful to anticipate test questions and to practice answering those questions.
4. Prior to taking a test, you should try to develop a positive state of mind.
5. It is very important to read the directions and test questions very carefully.
6. Answer the easy questions first.
7. Answer every item unless there is a penalty for guessing.
8. After you have completed the test, proofread the answers.
9. You can learn much from previous tests.
10. Each type of test question is different, and poses unique problems.

Teacher: "I hope everyone is prepared for today's test!"

Notes

CHAPTER 7

WRITING ASSIGNMENTS

Overview

Teachers differ widely in what they consider to be good writing. But there are certain basic principles that should be applied in most writing assignments. You should select a topic in which you are interested. Once you have done this, it is important to narrow down your topic.

In research type papers, the next step is to gather information about your topic. This is either done by going to the library or collecting some kind of data. While you are doing this, you should be thinking about the general content of your paper. I call this the incubation period. It is important not to rush into writing before you are prepared to do so. The information should be properly organized into an outline or structure before you actually begin your first draft. This serves as a plan.

After completing these preparatory steps, you can write the first draft. It is wise to let it sit awhile before making any revisions. When you feel that the time is appropriate, then you can make any desired revisions and corrections. Reading is one of the keys to good writing.

Selecting and narrowing your topic

If you have a choice, you should choose a topic that interests you. That should be the major factor you consider in selecting a topic. You could select something that you have been interested in for a long time. Then your paper could serve two purposes: it would help satisfy course requirements and satisfy your curiosity.

Once you have selected your topic, it is important to **NARROW IT DOWN**. Make it as specific as possible. For example, the topic "Life" is much too general. Something like "The educational problems of Samoan migrants" is more specific. However, the second topic might be too specific if you only have access to limited library facilities. The narrower the topic is, the better your chances of covering it thoroughly. Some teachers demand that you have a thesis or subject that is worded in a certain way.

Gathering information

One of the most frustrating things about writing is not having enough information to write about. You can avoid this situation by gathering information thoroughly before beginning to write. When you find a book on the topic, look through it (scan) to make certain that it has information about your specific topic. One way to do this quickly is to look at the **INDEX** in the back of the book or the **CONTENTS**.

As you gather information, take notes and keep them as **ORGANIZED** as possible. Organized notes will make it easier for you to write the paper. You will then know exactly where to find the information that you need. Make sure that the information you are getting is related to your topic.

The incubation period

After you have collected the necessary information, it is wise to let some time elapse before you begin to write. You need time to think about the various relationships and meanings of your data. You will not be able to do this if you write your papers in one sitting. There should be an **INCUBATION PERIOD** in which your ideas have the opportunity to develop. During this period you will think about different aspects of the topic. Don't rush this period, because it is crucial to the quality of your paper. Record your thoughts during this time. Sometimes a new thought might involve additional research. You should be willing to learn as much as possible on your topic. The incubation period allows you to fully develop your ideas.

Making an outline

Before you begin to write, you should make a detailed plan or outline. This outline will make writing much easier and less frustrating. You will flow through the writing if you have a plan to follow. A well developed plan will actually take some of the load off of your thinking so that you can devote your full attention to writing. The planning stage is when you decide which order the information will be discussed. There are times when an outline is more of a restriction than a help. Be willing to modify your outline if the information does not fit well into your original plan.

Writing the first draft

Some people find this aspect of writing to be the most difficult. Once it is done, then the rest is just a matter of revision. At some point you will feel ready to write. If you have done the proper preparation, then this will not be too difficult. By using your information and outline you have a good idea of your direction.

Your first draft does not have to be perfect. In fact, it is better to get some momentum going rather than trying to worry too much about wording. You can change that during your revisions. The important thing is to get the main ideas down so you can have something from which to work.

Using the dictionary

If you are uncertain about the spelling or meaning of a word, then use the dictionary. It might take a little bit of extra time, but it is worth the trouble. Misspellings and inappropriate words create a negative impression with most teachers. Besides, they can be avoided. There is no reason for having any mistakes. You should make a habit of writing with a dictionary near you.

Using the thesaurus

A thesaurus assists you when you are searching for different words and ways to say things. Your writing will seem fresher and more original when you don't use the same word excessively.

Making revisions and additions

After you have written the first draft, you should let it sit on the shelf for awhile. When you are ready, you can begin to make desired revisions. You should be willing to make changes. You need to be able to admit that you used the wrong word, didn't support a statement, or need to add or omit something. Consider your work as another person might; be your own critic.

You might come to the conclusion that you need to add some more information or examples. If you make a practice of double or triple-spacing your first draft, then corrections are easier to make.

Reading: the key to good writing

Few writers are truly original. As I am writing this, I am using bits and pieces of the many writers that I have read in my life. It would be impossible for me to write if I had never read a book.

Reading gives you many ideas about the way to phrase something. It also provides you with different ways of organizing material. The more you read, the easier it will be for you to write. Pay attention as you read. Your spelling and vocabulary will improve. That will aid in the quality of your writing. It is wise to learn from others and to borrow methods and ideas. The key to good writing is **PRACTICE**. **YOU LEARN TO BECOME A GOOD WRITER BY WRITING**.

*"Can I be a week late with
my history paper?"*

CHAPTER SUMMARY

1. You should select a topic that you are interested in.
2. It is important to narrow your topic.
3. Gathering information should precede any attempts to write a paper.
4. During the incubation period, you develop your ideas and think of different ways to put the paper together.
5. Before you begin to write, you should organize the information into an outline or structure. This will serve as a basic plan.
6. Writing the first draft should take place after you have completed the preparatory steps.
7. After you have written the first draft, you should make necessary revisions and additions.
8. Reading is one of the major keys to good writing.
9. The key to good writing is practice.
10. Use the dictionary and thesaurus to assist you with words.

CHAPTER 8

FOR THAT EXTRA EDGE

Overview

This chapter contains additional hints that did not fit into any of the previous chapters. Think about each one of them carefully. Where you sit in class can have an influence on how much you learn. It is usually better to sit toward the front of the room.

It is very important to attend every class and to be on time. The way you schedule your classes should be based upon your typical body time. Study groups can be useful because they use the principle of active learning.

Confidence and mental set can have a powerful influence on whether you succeed or fail in school. Course outlines should be read carefully, because they contain valuable information about the course and the teacher. Tape recorders are useful as a back-up to note-taking. It is important to know how to approach instructors. Your ability to contribute to class discussions is vital to academic success.

Seat selection

Where you sit in class can have a tremendous influence on how much you learn in that class. In general, it is better to sit toward the front of the room. This seating serves several purposes:
1. You can hear the teacher better.
2. You will have more of a tendency to pay attention.
3. You will find it easier to participate in class discussions or ask questions. This is especially true if you tend to be shy, because you won't notice people looking at you.
4. You are less likely to be bored.
5. The teacher will notice you more than if you are in the rear of the room.

It is usually better not to sit near individuals who are likely to distract you with jokes, comments, or notes. You are in the classroom to learn. You can pursue your social life somewhere else. In a discussion class, you might want to sit more in the middle of the room in order to establish eye contact with other students. However, in some cases you don't have a choice of where you sit. Try different locations until you find the one that is most comfortable for you.

Attendance and promptness

Attend every class and arrive on time. It is preferable to arrive a few minutes before class begins to make certain that you are prepared. Have your notebook open and pen ready before the teacher begins. It is too easy to lose the continuity of a lecture of course by irregular attendance.

If you arrive late or leave early, you actually miss more than just a few minutes. This is because teachers often make their most important points at the beginning or end of class. The beginning might include an overview which provides a clue to the main points to be covered. It could also include an important review or synopsis of the previous lecture.

The end of class could be the hurried completion of a lecture or the summary of the important points. Assignments and test dates are often made during the last few minutes of class. You are responsible for every minute of class. If you miss part or all of a class, it is *YOUR RESPONSIBILITY* to find out what happened during that period of time. You should get your information from a reliable person. Sometimes even by getting the notes from another person, you still miss the first-hand experience of seeing and hearing what the teacher said. There is no substitute for regular class attendance and attention.

Scheduling of classes

The way you schedule your classes (if you have a choice in the matter) is vitally important. Basically, you should make a schedule that is in accordance with your typical body time and work schedule (if you have one). If you are typically a late riser, it is not advisable to schedule your most difficult classes in the early morning. On the other hand, an early riser might want to complete the most difficult classes before noon. Don't over-load your schedule and expect to give all of your classes enough time and effort. You need plenty of time in order to learn properly. This is especially true of courses in your major field of study.

If you have a real problem managing your time, set up a schedule that forces you to be at school long enough to complete your work. Try to be near your best study environ-ment. One useful method is to schedule your classes far enough apart so that you can study each one immediately before and after the class. You could preview before class in order to get prepared for class. After class could be used for re-writing and re-organizing your notes, doing assignments, and otherwise finishing tasks related to the class. Experiment with different schedules until you find one that works for you.

Study groups

Studying in groups can be a valuable and enjoyable experience. First of all, you have the opportunity to **RECITE** the material. Secondly, you can ask questions about things you don't understand. Sometimes it is easier to ask a fellow student than it is to ask the teacher. Thirdly, you can hear other students explain the various concepts. You can share your ideas and receive feedback on them.

However, you can waste time by studying in groups. The most common reason is that students tend to socialize rather than focusing on the subject matter. You need to know when it is time to get back to the subject. Another problem is when you study in groups before studying on your own. This can weaken your confidence and cause some bad feelings among students who have studied on their own. There is a time to study on your own and time to study in groups. The important thing to consider is whether you are gaining some benefits from the experience.

Mental set

Mental set is a belief that you can or can't do something. Some people can't remember things primarily because they have convinced themselves that they aren't able to remember. They are so certain that they can't remember that it impairs their concentration and will to remember. Mental set can be a severe block to learning. As long as you are convinced that you can't do something, it is likely that you won't do it. Instead, use your energy to practice different methods and break your old habits and patterns.

Mental set could be considered in a positive sense also. You can develop **CONFIDENCE** and the belief that you can learn, remember, and succeed in school. The more you believe in your own ability to do something, the better you will be able to do it. Along with this confidence should come practice and the willingness to **CHANGE HABITS**.

103

Course outlines

At the beginning of most courses, the teacher will provide each student with a course outline or syllabus. This outline can provide you with some valuable information about the teacher and the course. When read carefully, it can indicate some of the following things:

1. The amount of work required in the course.
2. Expectations of the teacher such as promptness and class participation.
3. The sequence of topics to be covered.
4. Due dates.
5. The requirements of the course.

In some cases a course outline will give you information about whether the teacher is organized, more concerned with general or specific information, and other things.

Tape recorders

The primary value of tape recorders is that they allow you to get a complete verbal record of a class. However, their value can be lessened when other facts are considered. They include the following:

1. It tends to be boring to re-listen to an entire class.
2. It is time-consuming to do so.
3. If you rely on the tape recorder to listen for you, you might not pay attention or ever develop any skill in note-taking.
4. You are dependent upon the tape recorder's mechanical reliability. There is a chance that it might have some type of problem that could cause you to panic.
5. Some teachers do not like students to use them.

Approaching instructors

One of the keys to doing well in school is to establish some type of relationship with your teachers. The more you know them and feel comfortable with them, the easier it will be for you to learn from them. If you feel that your teachers are doing a good job, tell them so. Teachers need to know when they are getting their ideas across to students.

The other side of this issue is more difficult to handle. That is, what do you do when you are having problems with a teacher? This will depend upon several factors. Before approaching an instructor with a complaint or criticism, look at the entire situation honestly. Try to understand their point of view in the case. There is nothing worse for getting results than to begin by putting someone on the defensive by verbally attacking them.

After you have looked at the situation **OBJECTIVELY**, then make an appointment to see the teacher or try to catch them before or after class. Timing is crucial. You want to see them when they are in a receptive mood. Perhaps the best way to approach someone with negative comments is to begin by telling the teacher something that you like about his or her teaching. By doing this you are softening the blow of your criticism or complaint. Then **TACTFULLY** present your position. Listen carefully to the teacher's point of view. Be prepared with examples or you won't be very convincing. Be direct and get to the point. Be willing to compromise if necessary. The exact procedure will vary depending upon the situation.

Class discussions

In some classes you are evaluated more on your verbal ability than on your skills in memory, test-taking, and writing. It is quite important to be able to express yourself orally. The following principles should be considered in class discussions:
1. Listen carefully to others.
2. Try not to be repetitive. Instead, attempt to expand upon what others say.
3. Use fact and examples to support your statements whenever possible.
4. Read the assigned material prior to coming to class.
5. Think before you speak, and be selective in your comments. Be concerned with quality rather than quantity.
6. Don't interrupt others while they are speaking.

The Study Skills Graduate

CHAPTER SUMMARY

1. Where you sit in a class can have a major influence on how much you learn in that class.
2. It is vitally important to attend every class and to be prompt for class.
3. The way you schedule your classes should be based upon your typical work patterns and "body time."
4. Study groups can be useful if you take into account some of the possible drawbacks.
5. Mental set can have both a positive and negative effect on various academic skills.
6. Course outlines should be studied carefully for the information that they contain.
7. Tape recorders are primarily beneficial as a back-up to listening and note-taking rather than a substitute for them.
8. It is important to know when, where, and how to approach various instructors.
9. You should take care in criticizing your teachers.
10. The ability to contribute to class discussions can greatly affect your academic achievement.

SELF-EXAMINATION CHECKLIST

As you strive to improve your study skills, ask yourself the following questions:

1. Am I organized?
2. Am I wasting time and energy? If so, when and why?
3. Am I making the most of classroom time and learning as much as I possibly can in each class?
4. Am I taking the time to preview material before coming to class?
5. Am I trying to increase my vocabulary?
6. Am I anticipating test quetions and practicing answers to the questions?
7. Am I asking questions if I don't understand something?
8. Am I allowing myself enough time per subject?
9. Am I spending more time on difficult subjects or avoiding them?
10. Am I taking notes on the main points and major ideas?
11. Am I being an active learner by writing, reciting, and thinking about the material to be learned?
12. Am I learning as much as I possibly can about each of my teachers?
13. Am I spending too much time worrying about school and not enough time studying?
14. Am I trying to develop a positive attitude toward school?
15. Am I paying attention and concentrating to the best of my ability?
16. Am I trying different methods to see which ones work for me?
17. Am I rewarding myself for accomplishing tasks?
18. Am I trying to learn as much as I can about each of my subjects?
19. Am I studying on a regular basis?
20. Am I learning as much as I can about myself?
21. Am I trying to relate new material to what I already know?
22. Am I listening carefully to what the teacher is saying?
23. Am I taking initiative in pursuing knowledge?
24. Am I using as many senses as possible?
25. Am I doing my very best?

Notes

Abbreviations – ways of shortening words to make note-taking easier

Acronyms – using the first letter of words to assist in remembering them; e.g., IRS, USA, USSR, VIP

Active learning – using as many of your senses as possible in order to learn things

Associations – using what you already know to help you to learn and remember new material

Attention – focusing your senses upon the material to be learned

Attitude – the way that you think and feel about something; a positive attitude is necessary for academic success

Body time – the time or times at which you are able to perform certain tasks better

Concentration – directing your full attention on something; not being distracted by noise, thoughts, or feelings

Condense – to reduce material into fewer words; aids in memory

Cornell method – a special method of note-taking in which you divide the paper into sections; includes recording, reducing, reciting, reflecting, and reviewing

Efficiency – the ability to accomplish the most work in the least amount of time with the least effort

Grouping – placing material into meaningful categories in order to make it easier to learn and memorize

Handwritten textbook – getting your notes into the form of a book for study and review

Incubation period – in writing, the period in which you let your thoughts develop on a subject

Initiative – doing something without being told when and how to do it; taking control of and responsibility for your own education

Link method – a memory technique in which you make bizarre connections between successive words in a list to form a story

Location – using the location of something to assist in memory; e.g., the ancient Greek orators using the items in buildings to help them remember their speeches

Main ideas – the central or major concepts in a given subject; this is what you should be determining in lectures and books

Master calendar – a centralized listing of all due dates, test dates, and other important dates

Mental set – the belief that you can or cannot do something

Mnemonic devices – various techniques that aid in memory

Momentum – having direction and being in a productive work pattern or session

Note-taking – writing down the important material from lectures, discussions, and readings for later study and review; aids greatly in learning and memory

Organization – having an outline or pattern; refers to both personal study areas and the material to be learned; central to learning and memory

Previewing – reading or skimming the material to be covered prior to coming to class

Reflect – to think about

Rituals – preparatory activities that help us to get ready to perform certain tasks; e.g., cleaning off desk, having a drink

Scanning – looking for a specific piece of information rather than reading a book completely

Skimming – reading through material quickly for main ideas

Study skills – attitudes, processes, and methods that aid in learning and memory

BIBLIOGRAPHY

Adler, Mortimer J., and Van Doren, Charles. *How to read a book*. Rev. ed. New York: Simon and Schuster, 1972.

Armstrong, William H. *Study is hard work*. New York: Harper and Brothers Publishers, 1956.

Bliss, Edwin C. *Getting things done: the ABC's of time-management*. New York: Charles Scribner, 1976.

Brechner, Irv. *The college survival kit*. New York: Bantam Books, 1979.

Finkel, Lawrence S. and Krawltz, Ruth. *How to study and improve test-taking skills*. 2nd ed. Dobbs Ferry, N.Y.: Oceana, 1976.

Funk, Wilfred, and Lewis, Norman. *30 days to a more powerful vocabulary*. Rev. ed. New York: Funk and Wagnalls, 1970.

Gross, Michael. *The how to go to college book*. Seattle: Passage Publishing, 1979.

James, D.E. *Student's guide to efficient study*. New York: Pergamon Press, 1967.

McKowen, Clark. *Get your A out of college*. Los Altos: William Kaufmann, Inc., 1981.

Millman, Jason, and Pauk, Walter. *How to take tests*. New York: McGraw-Hill, 1969.

Pauk, Walter. *How to study in college*. Boston: Houghton Mifflin, 1962.

Shaw, Harry. *30 ways to improve your grades*. New York: McGraw-Hill, 1969.

Strunk, William, and White, E.B. *The elements of style*. New York: Macmillan Company, 1977.